Why Can't We Live Together?

The Kid-Sized Answer To A King-Sized Question About Divorce

WRITTEN BY: MADISON AND LUCAS LOVATO
ILLUSTRATIONS BY: TIM ACOSTA

Copyright© 2018 Lori Lehew

Dedicated to Nana JoAnn.

She always helps us in every way possible!

Thank you!

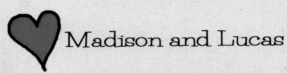Madison and Lucas

Have you ever **wondered why** you and your parents **don't live together** in the same house like other families?

Hi, I'm Lucas. My sister Madison and I **wondered** the **same thing.** But we know that every family is different.

Some families have a
grandma living with them.
Other families only
have a Mom or a Dad.

Some kids are adopted
by families who just want to
love them and take
care of them.

Our mom and dad are
divorced and they
each **live** in a
different house.

We liked it **better** when we all
lived together in the
same house.

Our Mom says that families
are special because they all
look different.

She says that it's **love** that
makes a family, not
where you live.

But **why** does your parents being **divorced** mean that families have to live in **separate houses?**

Our mom says it's because my
Dad is pizza and she
is ice cream.

I love pizza and ice cream, but what do my Mom and Dad have to do with that?

Then my Mom asked me if I ever thought of putting ice cream on top of my pizza?

Cheese pizza and mint chocolate chip
ice cream are my favorites,
but pizza and ice cream
together yuck!!

That's when my Mom told Madison and I that **she** and my **Dad** are like **pizza** and **ice cream.**

Pizza and ice cream may **not** be
good together, but I can
still love them both.

The **same is true** for my **Mom and Dad.** They may not be good together, but I can **still love each** of them.

Finding out your parents are getting a **divorce** and are going to **live apart** is **never easy.**

One thing is for sure! Your
parents love you, and
you love them, no matter
where you live.

Your family **may not look** like other families, but it is still a family. **Your family!**

happy
happy happy

FAMILY

Your family is made of love, happiness, smiles, and laughter, no matter where you live.

Remember, **lots of kids** have parents that are **divorced** and live in **different houses**.

They have **families** that **look** like yours and mine.

When you **meet other kids**
whose parents are divorced, be kind.
Let them know that
it's okay that their parents
don't live together.

Chances are that their parents are like pizza and ice cream too.

Tell Us How You Feel
It's time for us to help you feel better.

Dear Lucas and Madison:

When my parents told me that they weren't going to live in the same house anymore, I didn't know why.
I felt _____ because _____ .

But I know that all families are different. I know families that have _____ living with them. I also know families that live with _____ .

My favorite foods are _____ and _____ .
Just like pizza and ice cream, these foods would not taste good together, either.

I know that I can love both my Mom and my Dad. I am loved no matter where I live. My parents show me their love
by _____ and _____ .

When I meet kids whose parents don't live together I will be kind to them by _____ .

Thanks for listening!
From _____
City _____ State _____

What's For Dinner?

Art makes everyone happy! Draw a picture of what
two foods your parents are like.

Made in the USA
Lexington, KY
21 February 2019

Why Can't We Live Together?
reassuringly tells the story of a brother and sister who were
told that their Mom and Dad were no longer going to live
together because they were getting a divorce. The story
features the children speaking to the reader about their
confusion while providing an answer to this question that many
families can relate too.

The book works to comfort young readers with an easy,
child-friendly explanation about why their living arrangements
are changing. The book is uplifting and calming and engages
kids at the end to address questions about living with their
parents in two separate homes.

ISBN 9781983845390

90000

9 781983 845390